Don't Die
SURVIVE!

JOHNATHAN PETERS

How to Survive…

Disclaimer

The author and publisher disclaim any liability from any injury that may result from the use, proper or improper, of the information contained in this book.

Introduction

Life is full of dangers that can threaten to put an end to your existence if you don't have the knowledge to overcome them. This book will give you the run down on how to survive the wackiest to most life-threatening situations so you can walk away to tell the tale. You may think you will never find yourself in any of these situations, but can you guarantee it? Wouldn't it be better to have this information and never need it, than to need the information and not have it?

Read through this book and commit the information to memory. The next time you find yourself at the beach and you get stung by a jellyfish, or you are at the bank and a gunman walks in, you will know exactly what to do to survive.

An Avalanche

The first step is to be aware of what is happening around you. Before you go skiing or into an area where an avalanche is a possibility, invest in a beacon. This is what can save your life. The beacon emits a signal that will help rescuers find you, even if you are buried under several feet of snow.

If the avalanche has already started and the snow is tossing you around like a rag doll, do what you can to climb up. Try to ride the wave of snow so you are close to the top. It isn't going to be easy, but you have to try. You will also want to try to keep one arm up over your head, like you are raising your hand for the teacher. This will help rescuers spot you and give you an idea of which way to dig.

If the snow has buried you, your face is going to be pressed into the snow. Use your warm spit to melt the area around your mouth and nose to create an air pocket that will allow you to breathe. As you create a bigger hole, note the direction your spit falls. If it falls back in your face, you know you are facing the sky and can start digging. If it falls down, you are face down and need to try to maneuver your body to dig the other way.

Lastly, DO NOT PANIC! Do not let the claustrophobia take over. This will reduce your chances of survival. Keeping your breathing regulated will preserve the air pocket you have carved out with your spit. It will also help you think rationally about your current situation.

A Stampeding Crowd

A stampeding crowd is more common than one would think. The stampede can happen at any time and only takes a single person to set off a panic that elicits the flight instinct in humans. It is very easy to trip and fall to the ground when that flight instinct takes over. This can be deadly as people stomp on you in their mass exodus without a care in the world for anybody around them.

If you are to survive a stampeding crowd, you need to stay on your feet. Don't try to go against the flow of the crowd. Keep your feet on the ground and walk or run with the crowd. Slowly try to make your way to the edge of the crowd so you can get out. While doing so, keep your arms up and in front of your chest. This will allow you to balance yourself and keep some space between you and the people around you.

Do not shout or scream. If you are with somebody, use your eyes or basic sign language to communicate. Remember, you are in a crowd of people you want to break away from. You don't want them to follow you. Do not give in to the urge to scream and push against the crowd. Go with the flow and calmly look for a way out.

A Vicious Dog Attack

If a dog attacks you, you will likely have the urge to panic, shout, and run. All three of these things could get you seriously injured or even killed.

If a growling dog approaches you, stay still. Don't run away, don't move, and don't shout out at it. Slowly look around to see what you can grab to put between you and the dog should an attack occur. A stick is your best friend in a dog attack. You can lodge it between the dog's mouth and your arm or leg, smack the dog on the nose with it to get it to stop, or jam it down the dog's throat. This will make the jaws unclench and give you the chance to break free.

If a dog has your arm or leg, do not try pulling it back. This will result in tears in your skin and you will suffer more than you would from a few puncture wounds. Use your free arms and legs to get the dog off you.

Do what you can to stay standing. If you don't have a stick, you can shove your hand down the dog's throat to get them to stop. A few bites are better than an all-out mauling.

You can completely avoid being attacked by a dog by avoiding its territory. Should you be forced to enter a dog's territory, and they approach you, don't make any sudden movements. Lastly, try using a calm but firm voice and order the dog to sit, stay, or stop. If you're lucky, the dog will understand these basic commands.

A Riptide

A day at the beach can quickly turn into a nightmare if you happen to find yourself caught in a riptide. Riptides are not easily seen and you won't notice what is happening until it is too late and you are sucked in.

If you find yourself being pulled into a riptide, take a deep breath and get ready to swim for your life. Do not attempt to go straight for the beach. You need to swim parallel to the beach. Swim using long strokes until you are out of the riptide. Once you have put some distance between you and the riptide, head for the beach.

If you cannot swim out of the riptide, float on your back or tread water. Switching back and forth will help keep you afloat while you wait for help to arrive. Yell for help and wave an arm in the air to attract attention.

A Nuclear Explosion

A nuclear explosion is devastating. It is one disaster that has the ability to destroy an entire population. The explosion, however, is nothing compared to the fallout. The radiation resulting from the blast will remain in the air, ground, and water for days, weeks, and, even years following the explosion.

If you are within a five-mile radius of a nuclear bomb detonation, your chances of survival are slim-to-none. Every mile outside of that five mile radius increases your chances of survival. While, the government will tell you to shelter in place if there is the threat of a nuclear explosion you really want to be as far from the epicenter of the explosion as possible.

You do want to seek shelter and quickly, but your standard home may not be enough. If you are stuck and your house is the only shelter available, tape plastic over every window, door and vent. You don't want any air from the outside coming in. Ideally, a basement is your best bet. You want lots of cement between you and the fallout that happens after the bomb detonates.

If possible, seek shelter upwind of the epicenter. Radiation will travel with the wind so you don't want to be directly in it's path. If you don't have a basement, but know where you can find one that is less than five minutes away, head that way as soon as you hear the boom. If you make it, the basement will increase your chance of survival.

Survival in the days following a nuclear explosion will be difficult. Do what you can to avoid being outside. This will decrease your exposure to radiation. The radiation will dissipate overtime, however, depending on the size of the explosion and your proximity to it, it can take years. Have a plan to leave everything behind and head away from the blast zone.

Falling Into a Frozen Lake

Walking across a frozen lake is dangerous. Ideally, you want to completely avoid doing so if you are not sure about the thickness of the ice. Even then, there may be places where the ice is thin and an accident is inevitable. If you happen to fall through the ice, don't panic and don't gulp air. Your body's response will be to gasp when the cold water hits you, but fight it. You don't want to take in any water.

Although you may feel like every second is putting you that much closer to death, you actually have between about 15 minutes and 45 minutes to get out of the water and still go on to live a normal life. Try to keep that in mind as you plan your escape.

Your first step towards escape is to get yourself back to the hole that you fell through or look for another hole in the ice if the current has moved you. Once you find a hole, place you elbows up onto the ice and let your body float. This will make it easier to crawl out of the water. Kick your feet in the water to give yourself some momentum to get up on the ice. Once you have gotten on the ice, roll away from the hole to help distribute your weight and avoid creating another crack or hole.

If you cannot get out of the ice, relax, hold on to the ice and call for help. Waving a hand in there will help others see you. Don't waste your energy by thrashing about.

A Hostage Situation

A hostage situation is something that can occur at any time in your life. It may be something as mundane as running into the gas station to get a gallon of milk and finding yourself smack in the middle of a robbery. You could be taken hostage. You may be at the bank, at work, or simply sitting in your car, and you could be taken hostage by a desperate person.

Being a hostage is scary—there is no doubt about it. Only someone who has no regard for your life would take you as a hostage, which makes you disposable. You have to change that. Do not become a nuisance. Do not talk unless spoken to. Stay calm and watch and listen to everything happening around you. Look for doors and windows if you are on a ground floor. Note whether the hostage taker has a gun and which hand they are holding it in.

Do not shout or plead with the hostage taker. If you are given the chance to talk to the police, only give yes or no answers. Do not try to give out more information than the hostage taker is willing to allow. Basically, don't press your luck.

Do what you can to stay low to the ground. You don't want to be in the way of a police sniper's shot if and when it comes. If police bust through the door, they are going to be aiming high where the hostage taker is likely standing. Do not make any sudden movements or appear threatening to the person. If you have a serious medical condition, like asthma or diabetes, let the hostage taker know. If you die, you are not of any value to the person.

Realize that trying to escape your situation increases your odds of being killed or seriously injured. Do not attempt to do so if there is a chance you will be seen. If your hostage taker has a gun, you cannot outrun a bullet. You must be watchful and wait for the perfect opportunity. In many situations, hostages are freed once the hostage-taker gets what they want or the police manage to disarm or kill them. It may take hours, but your patience is what will likely save your life.

A Severe Lightning Storm

Lightning storms are very common in the spring and summer months. As with anything, prevention is the key. If you see dark clouds rolling in or the weatherman has reported there is a risk of severe storms, take shelter. Stay home and don't venture outside.

If you are home when the severe storm blows in, there are some things you need to do to stay safe while taking shelter:

1) Stay out of the tub or shower—electricity and water don't mix; don't do the dishes either.
2) Don't use your landline.
3) Don't hang out in front of a window or open the door to watch the storm.
4) Get off your desktop computer and avoid using anything that is plugged in (for
your sake, unplug your electronics to keep them from being fried).
5) Avoid standing next to a cement wall or lying on a concrete floor—the rebar can conduct electricity.

If you are caught outdoors when the storm rolls in, you need to find shelter immediately. If you are on a boat or near water—move. Avoid taking shelter under the tall trees in the area. Standing near a cluster of smaller trees is a better option. Lightning is attracted to the highest point; you don't want to be anywhere near that.

Avoid standing next to metal bars or fences that electricity can travel through. Do not stand on top of a hill or anything that makes you higher than everything in your surroundings. If you are out in the open, head for a valley or a ravine where you will be lower than surrounding objects.

Always try to find shelter instead of riding out the storm outdoors. A tent is not shelter. You need to shelter in a wooden building to have the best chance of avoiding being struck by lightning.

Being Lost in the Woods

So, you go out for a nice long walk in the woods and find yourself lost and confused. How do you get back? Do you try to find your way out and risk becoming even more lost or stay put and wait for someone to find you? Stay put. You are going to do more harm than good by trying to find your way out. Hopefully, you told somebody you were heading out for the day and when you would be back. They will sound the alarm and it will give searchers somewhere to start looking for you.

While you are waiting to be rescued, you should be in survival mode. You need clean drinking water, a fire if it is chilly, and shelter. Don't worry so much about food right away. Yes, you will be hungry, but you can survive several days (weeks really) without eating. The other three are your priority.

Always boil any water you collect from a stream or lake. This will kill anything in your water that can make you extremely ill. You can create a shelter out of sticks, branches and leaves or even stack some rocks to create a barrier between you and the elements. Do what you can to make your presence known. Lighting a fire and adding wet wood or grass will produce a lot of smoke. Blowing a whistle, if you have one, is also useful. If you have to move to find a better camp or grab some water, leave some trail markers. This will help you find your way back and let others know you were there.

Driving Your Car Into a Lake

It isn't something a person does intentionally, but accidents happen. Guardrails fail and bridges collapse. If you find yourself in a body of water and your car is heading towards the bottom with you in it, you have to act fast.

The first and most important step is to keep your wits about you. Roll down your windows as you are falling through the air or the second you make contact with the water. If you have your seatbelt on, get it off immediately. The car will sink front end first. While you may be inclined to jump in the back seat and hide in the pocket of air that will be there, this is a waste of time. You need to get out quickly.

If you didn't get the windows down before the car was submerged, you will need to break out the window. Don't go for the windshield; it is made with a durable material that will not shatter. Go for side windows. Even they will be difficult to break while under water. Don't give up. Use anything you can find in your car to bust the window. Because this kind of accident can and does happen, it is a good idea to keep a and ExiTool in the glove-box of your car. It is a seatbelt cutter on one end and the other will shatter your windshield with little effort.

A Tornado

Tornadoes are loud and destructive and can flatten an entire city in a matter of seconds. Every year, these frightening storms kill people who are either not expecting the storm and are unable to find shelter, or don't know what to do.

Take shelter somewhere below ground. A basement is always your best option. A root cellar works as well. If you don't have a basement, take the following steps:

1) Find a room without windows or get as far from the windows as possible.
2) Stay on the ground floor.
3) Hide under a stairwell or in the bathroom in the tub.
4) Cover your body with a mattress if you can or hold a pillow over your head and wrap yourself up in a thick blanket.

If you are in your car when you see a tornado or hear the sirens, you need to find shelter. If you cannot make it to a safe shelter, keep your seatbelt on, cover your body with a blanket and lie across the seat. It is helpful to find a depressed area, like a ditch or valley. Anything that is lower than the ground around you will increase your odds of survival as the tornado goes right over the top of you.

An Earthquake

When you feel the ground start to tremble, don't panic. Find shelter under a sturdy table or desk and wait for the shaking to stop. Fortunately, earthquakes are over in a matter of seconds with the largest over in less than two minutes. If you can't find a table or sturdy desk, drop to all fours and tuck your head, and place your hands over it to protect it from falling debris. Do not run outside or try to escape from where you are. You won't have time. Avoid sheltering next to windows, as the glass will shatter and cut you.

If you are outside when the shaking starts, try to get away from any tall buildings, trees, and structures. You don't want them coming down on top of you. Get to an open space and drop to your knees. Standing in a strong earthquake is like trying to stand on Jell-O. You risk getting serious injured by trying to remain upright.

If you are in a car, pull over and wait for the earthquake to stop. Avoid parking next to tall buildings and trees. Do not stop on a bridge or under an overpass because they may collapse.

A Hurricane

Fortunately, hurricanes are one of those things that you will get plenty of advanced warning about. They don't just sneak up on you. Ideally, you don't want to be in the path of a hurricane. If you can't avoid it, then you will hopefully have a sturdy shelter to take cover in and the necessary supplies to shelter in place for at least 12 hours.

If you must shelter at home, find a closet. If you don't have a closet, the corner of a room is the next best thing. You want to be away from windows that may break from the force of the wind. Turn off the main water and gas line to your home to avoid a mess should the lines rupture. You may also be instructed to shut off the main breaker to your home. Know where these are beforehand.

Flooding

Flooding is typically the result of a major storm, but it isn't going to just happen. There will be some sort of warning sign, and you should be ready for it. If you are at home, shut off the main power, gas and water line. Get out and head for higher ground.

If you are caught in a flood, do what you can to get out of the rushing water. Climb a tree, get on the roof of your house, or take the stairs to the roof of your apartment building. The water is deadly, and the debris floating in the water can be even deadlier. The water may also be electrified if live power lines have fallen.

Never attempt to drive through standing water. You never know how deep it is. If it disables your car, you could be trapped.

A Building on Fire

If you hear the fire alarm go off while working on the tenth floor of a building, you need to get out in a hurry. Obviously, never take the elevator. Electricity will be going out and you will be trapped in a burning box.

If you see flames or smoke, get down and crawl as quickly as you can to the stairwell. In many cases, the stairwells will be free from smoke due to the heavy doors that seal the areas from the main halls. Run down the stairs. Never open a door to a new floor without checking it first. Feel the door and the handle: if it is hot, don't open the door. Listen for firefighters and be prepared to answer and follow their instructions.

An Active Shooter Situation

Active shooters are becoming far too common in this day and age. If you are at the mall, school, or at work, and a gunman opens fire, you only have seconds to react. If you are in a room and can hear shooting, shut the door, lock it and barricade it.

If you are in an open area, look for an escape route. Be prepared to make your move when the shooter is distracted. Hide under a desk, behind a door, or anything you can find—even a person who has already been shot and succumbed to their wounds. Stay quiet and turn off your cell phone to avoid attracting attention.

If the shooter spots you and is coming towards you, fight. Yell, scream, and attack with everything you have. You may still be shot, but you have a better chance of taking the shooter out if you fight back.

Falling Down a Mountainside

If you happen to slip and fall while climbing a mountain or hillside, your first reaction will be to reach and grab something to hold onto. Do it. Grab roots, trees or rocks and hold on. Even if the roots give out, you will slow your fall. Continue to do this all the way down. This will gradually slow your fall.

Do what you can to slide down on your back. This gives you a better chance of landing on your feet when you reach the bottom. Try to keep your knees bent as you approach the bottom. When you hit the bottom, if you've managed to land on your feet, you will still fall. Throw your body to the side. You don't want to fall on your back or risk smashing your head when you fall forward.

A Capsized Ship

If you are on a ship that is capsizing, you only have seconds to take action. Get away from the ship until it has completely rolled. Jump away from the ship and swim as far as you can to avoid getting hit by the ship as it rolls.

Be cautious and avoid getting tangled up in any rigging, nets, or lines that may be attached to the boat. There is a good chance the capsized ship will hold your weight if you can climb on top. This will help keep you out of the water, which is especially important if the water is cold. Stay with the boat to increase your odds of being seen by air rescue or a passing ship. If you managed to get into the lifeboat, it will act as a beacon for searchers.

A Jellyfish Sting

If you are swimming in the ocean and encounter a jellyfish prepare to be in a great deal of pain if you get stung. If you get stung, get out of the water and immediately take action. Do not pee on your sting. That is a myth and it doesn't work. Use a towel or stick to remove the tentacle from your body if it is attached. Do not touch it with your bare hands.

Saltwater from the ocean should be poured over the area. Fresh water can actually make the pain worse. You may need to take a dose of Benadryl if you start to have swelling or redness all over your body. You can help ease the sting by mixing a paste of meat tenderizer (found in the spice aisle at your grocery store) and water. Smooth the paste over the area and let it sit until the stinging subsides.

A Snake Bite

If you get bitten by a snake, you don't have much time to respond before the venom begins coursing through your bloodstream. You need to immobilize the limb. Use a splint if needed. Loosen any clothing around the area and take off watches or rings if the bite is on your hand.

Put pressure on the area of the bite. Use your belt or a shoestring to hold a bandage in place while you get to a hospital. If you have the luxury of being able to call for help, do so immediately and sit tight until they get to you. While you wait, lie down with the bite level with your body or below your heart. Do not cut the bite or suck the venom out, as this could be fatal.

Being Attacked in an Elevator

If you happen to find yourself in an elevator with a violent individual, you must be prepared to defend yourself and neutralize the threat. Basic self-defense moves will come in handy here. One of the most effective moves is to hit the nose of your attacker with the outside edge of the palm of your hand. Also, try poking their eyes with your fingers to debilitate them long enough for you to hit them in the gut or groin area with your knee.

These simple moves can stop an attacker in their tracks and give you time to stop the elevator on the closest floor and get off. Never stop the elevator between floors. You want to get out of the moving box and away from the attacker as quickly as possible.

A Long Fall

If you happen to be pushed off a cliff or find yourself skydiving with a parachute that won't deploy, you need to know how to fall the right way. Assuming you are free falling, do what you can to slow yourself by spreading your arms and legs wide. When you get close to the ground, tuck and roll. Keep your head protected by shielding it with your arms. Roll instead of trying to land on your feet. Trying to land on your feet will seriously injure you.

Crossfire

If you find yourself in the middle of a gunfight and don't want to get caught in the crossfire—get low and stay there. Do not make yourself an easy target. This means, don't stand or even crawling. Anybody trying to shoot somebody is going to be aiming high, not at the other person's toes, which is where you want to be.

Belly-crawl to avoid drawing a lot of attention to yourself. Do not threaten the shooter either. Once you are out of immediate danger, find a place to hide until the shooting has left.

Being Buried Alive

If you have found yourself buried alive, you need to stay calm. Do not get excited. That will cause you to use up any available air you have. You want to take shallow breaths that will keep your body oxygenated while conserving available oxygen. Every time you exhale, you are releasing carbon dioxide into the air, which is poisonous when you breath it back in.

Hopefully, you are in a very shallow grave that makes it possible for you to dig out. If you are in a box or a coffin, don't attempt to open it or punch a large hole over your face. It will fill with dirt and suffocate you. It is a good idea to try to get your shirt off to cover your face with it. Use your arms to push up. This will hopefully send the dirt to your feet while pushing the dirt off of your untimely grave.

Once you have a small hole leading to the surface, feel free to make some noise to alert someone to your presence. Do not yell if you don't have a clear path to the surface. Your voice will be muffled and you will waste oxygen.

A Pressure Washer Accident

If you are going about your business, using your pressure washer to clean the driveway or garage floor, you'd best be careful. They can be deadly. If you have been hit with a stream of water from a pressure washer, don't ignore it. Skin lesions can easily become infected. Clean it and have it looked at by a medical professional. Wearing proper eye protection can protect your eyes from flying objects that have been dislodged by the powerful spray. Avoid trying to move rubbish with the pressure washer as they can become dangerous, flying projectiles.

An Excruciating Winter

A brutal winter that brings frigid temperatures and serious snowstorms is tough to survive. Do what you can to stay warm by burning hard woods like fir and tamarack. Keep your family in one area of the home to conserve heat. Make sure you are paying attention to your home's roof during a snowstorm. Take the time to remove the snow from the roof to prevent the roof from collapsing.

Avoid working outdoors when it is extremely cold. If you must, protect your skin by wearing appropriate clothing. Cover your hands and nose and make sure your feet are warm and dry. Do not stay outside if you are even a little wet. Stay home and avoid driving when possible. If you must drive and end up stranded, stay in your car and wait for help.

A Car Crash

A seat belt will go a long ways to helping you survive a car crash. If you see a crash is imminent, put both hands on the steering wheel at the 9 and 3 position. This will keep your arms from getting caught in the airbag. Put your head against the headrest and straighten your arms. Do not bend your wrists.

Steer the car away from any large objects that you are headed for. When you stomp on the brakes, you will lose some of your ability to control the car. Only pump the brakes if you do not have an anti-lock brake system on your car. Do what you can to reduce your speed. The less speed you have, the less damaging the accident will be.

An Airplane Crash

Let's say that your plane is going down and you have about 30 seconds, possibly a minute or two to figure out how to survive. If you are on a commercial airplane, the little oxygen masks will drop from the ceiling. Remember that your seat doubles as a flotation advice and be mindful of where the nearest exits are.

When booking your flight, hopefully you booked your seat in the middle of the plane, near the wing section and within 5 rows of the exit door. This gives you the best odds for survival. Skip the window seat and opt for the aisle seat for an easier escape. Brace yourself with your head down between your knees. When the plane stops moving, you get moving. Don't wait to gather your wits. Get up and get out. A fire is a very likely side effect of a plane crash. You will only have about 90 seconds before the plane goes up in flames.

A Volcanic Eruption

An earthquake may trigger a volcano or it may erupt with little warning. If you are not at risk of being consumed by flowing lava, stay where you are. Close the doors and seal the windows. You must block all of the toxic air from the outside. Turn off your air conditioner as well. Do not go outside. If you must, cover your mouth and nose with a mask or a shirt. Breathing in ash is like breathing in cement dust. When it combines with the moisture in your lungs, you will have a solid mass in your lungs that will suffocate you.

Do not try to cross any places covered with black crust because molten lava lies below. It is likely extremely hot and can melt your shoes or car tires within seconds. Go around.

If you are in an area that is heavily covered in ash, you will need to check your roof to make sure it is not overloaded. Use a roof rake or shovel to remove the ash.

Being Held at Gunpoint

If you are being held up at gunpoint—don't be a hero. Heroes rarely survive. Give the person what they want. Do not be defiant or try to reason with the person. Listen to their instructions and remain calm. Keep your hands in the air and avoid making any sudden movement that might startle the person. Try to speak to the person only if they seem to be willing to listen. If they demand you stop talking, do so.

Pay attention to your surroundings. If you see help, be prepared to drop to the ground and allow your rescuer to do their job.

Being Robbed

Of course you don't want to lose the things you have worked so hard for, but they are nothing compared to your life. If you are being robbed, stay out of the way and let the robbers take what they want. Do not try to stop them or get in their way. If they have given you specific instructions to stay down or to keep your hands up, do so. Pay close attention to every detail about the robber, without being overly obvious. Notice their eye color, build and which hand they are holding their weapon in. Listen to the way they speak and make note of any names that are used during the robbery.

If you are asked for safe combinations or where the keys to the car are, provide the information. Stay calm and don't try to bargain with the robbers. The sooner they have robbed you, the sooner they will be gone.

A Street Fight

If you get caught in a street fight, remember, there are no rules. Do whatever you have to do to survive. Use your keys, purse, briefcase, or anything you can find. Fight until you can get away. Don't stick around once you have knocked your opponent to the ground or managed to blind them by poking their eyes. You are not trying to win a fight. You are trying to survive and that means escaping with your life.

A Raging Teenager

A raging hormonal teenager can be more terrifying than any of the other topics we have covered. They are irrational, loud and unpredictable. The only way to survive is to ride the wave. Let the kid know you are there when they are ready to talk, and be prepared to dole out some tough love. Never get into a battle of wits or pick a battle you cannot possibly win. Don't let a teenager anger you, or you will lose. Give them the space and time they need to cool down.

Conclusion

Human instinct is to survive, but sometimes, instinct isn't enough. With a little knowledge, you can survive the scenarios presented in this book and live to see another day. Some of these scenarios may seem far-fetched, but in this day and age, anything is possible. You may never expect to find yourself fighting for your life, but one day, you just might have to.